Overlooked
Undertakings

Overlooked Undertakings

Photographs by Audrey Heller

SQUINT
PICTURES

These photos are the fusion of the influences of Dr. Seuss, Edward Weston and Jacques Cousteau.

Dr. Seuss taught me that just because something is playful and absurd, doesn't mean it's not valuable and true.

Edward Weston showed me that "seeing" is partly what my eyes do, but mostly what my brain does.

And Jacques Cousteau invited me into a world where science is as dramatic as fiction.

When I was little, I was enthralled by the fantasy that we all might be tiny creatures in a giant's world. That idea was exciting and terrifying. Exciting because it meant that there was so much more to explore than anyone was letting on, and terrifying because we could be squashed at any moment.

I try to be like Horton, the elephant whose oversized ears helped him to find a civilization inside a dust speck, and pay attention to the small worlds around me.

The Apple

Challenging Conditions

Daily

Cafe Society

Double

Never Be Lonely Again!

Heart and Soul

Ultramarin

Fish Out of Water

Damage Control

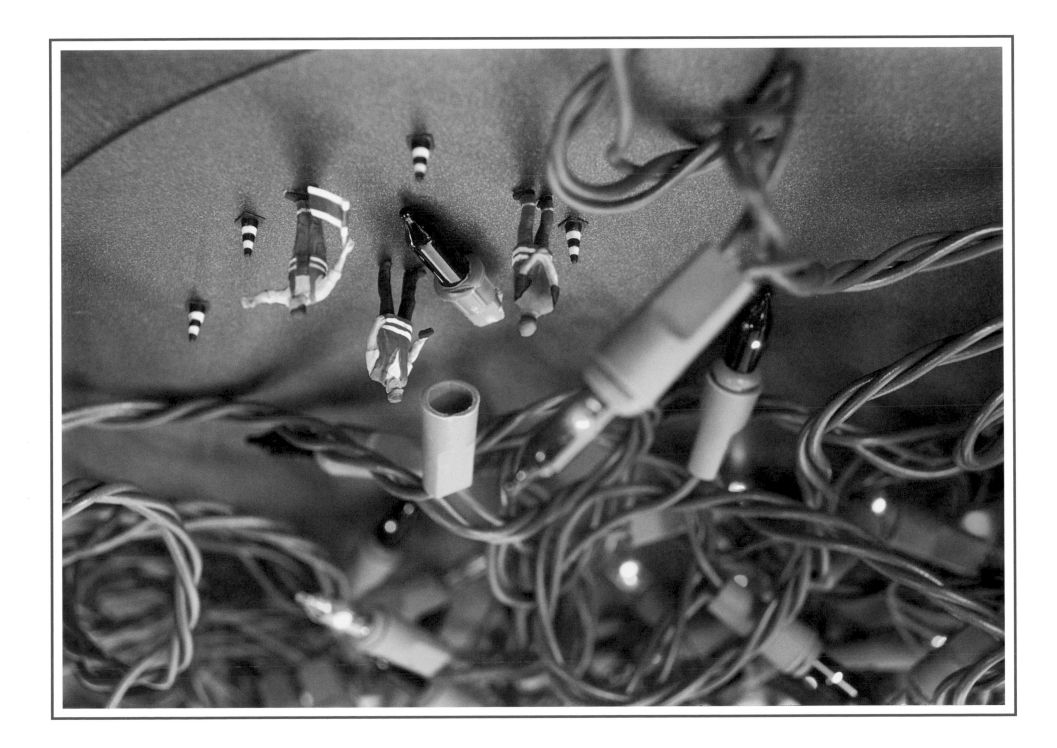

Sprout

Unfurl

What You Sow

Ripened

Lifesaver

Red Sea

Steady

Dry Spell

Two on One

Stardust

Wrap

Slinky

Spiro

End Well

Ascent

Concrete Evidence

California

Grand Tour

Sight

Shovel

Scrabble

Shift Freedom

Mother (Board) Earth

Liberty

Middle Path

Nurture Nature

The Work at Hand

Upkeep

Urban Culture

Three O'Clock

Rush Hour

Thief

Corked

Cloven

Curves

Near Perfect

Oom-pah

Ring of Fire

Jambalaya

Holes

Drive

Writer's Block

The Taming

Pet. Should ...

Kath. O slow-wing'd turtle, sha...
thee?

Pet. Ay, for a turtle, as he takes a buzzard.

Kath. Come, come, you wasp, i' faith you are too
angry.

Pet. If I be waspish, best beware my sting. 210

Kath. My remedy is then to pluck it out.

Pet. Ay, if the fool could find it where it lies.

Kath. Who knows not where a wasp does wear his
sting?

In his tail.

Kath. In his tongue. 215

Pet. Whose tongue?

Kath. Yours, if you talk of tales, and so farewell.

Pet. What, with my tongue in your tail? Nay,
come again,
Good Kate; I am a gentle... Th... ll try. *She strikes him.*

Kath. ... , if you strike again. 220

Pet. I swear I'll cuff you, if you strike again.

Kath. So may you lose your arms.
If you strike me, you are no gentleman,
And if no gentleman, why then no arms.

Pet. A herald, Kate? O, put me in thy books!

Kath. What is your crest? a coxcomb? 225

Pet. A combless cock, so Kate will be my hen.

Kath. No cock of mine, you crow too like a
craven.

Pet. Nay, come, Kate, come; you must not look
so sour.

Kath. It is my fashion when I see a crab. 230

... Why, here's no crab, and therefore look not
...

But thou w...
With gentle confere...
Why does the world report that...
O sland'rous world! Kate like...
Is straight and slender, and as br...
As hazel-nuts, and sweeter than...
O, let me see thee walk. Thou...

Kath. Go, fool, and whom...

Pet. Did ever Dian so beco...
As Kate this chamber with he...
O, be thou Dian, and let her...
And then let Kate be chaste...

Kath. Where did you st...

Pet. It is extempore, fr...

Kath. A witty mother!...

Pet. Am I not wise?

Kath. Yes, keep you...

Pet. Marry, so I m...
bed;
And therefore setting a...
Thus in plain terms: y...
That you shall be m...
And will you, nill y...
Now, Kate, I am a...
For by this light w...
Thy beauty that d...
Thou must be mar...
For I am he am b...
And bring you fr...
Conformable as...

Walkers

This book is dedicated to my parents,
Irene and Geoffrey Heller
who have never overlooked my undertakings.

Thanks

I am filled with gratitude for the many, many people who have helped, guided and prodded me along my way. Close friends and strangers have played equal roles, and I'm afraid to start with a list that will be grossly incomplete. But I will point to a few folks whose fingerprints are particularly identifiable in this book.

I'll start with you, since you're reading this. I am lucky that my work puts me in contact with so many encouraging voices. When it all seems too hard or too hot or too crazy to be toting my art around the country, one heart-felt smile refuels me. Thank you.

In my travels I have gathered a fine posse of colleagues who make life easier by sharing the load, literally and figuratively. Taking the prize for carrying the most weight are Chris and Kyle Dahlquist, without whom I would have tossed in the towel a while ago, and Joel Loughman, my summer anchor, whose generosity inspires me always.

Kristin Argue, who has been my comrade since we both cut 9th grade field hockey, helped me cut the first mats, and hang the first show, and has hung in ever since, helping me celebrate every new step and muddle through every misstep. I couldn't imagine a better friend.

Setting the bar high for making a business part of a community, are Keith Schroeder of Castro Photo and Mark Robyn of Robyn Color. If you enjoy this work, please make a point of supporting independent businesses. We all pay a huge price when they're gone.

I have had a lot of passing collaborators on these photos over the years.Thanks to Andy Bosch, Megan Bosch, Mark Finley, Bill Samios, Paul Hill and Paul Bostwick for flashlight holding, prop gathering and coffee styling.

This book has been floating in limbo for a long time, and some people get extra credit for keeping it bouyant. Nancy and Tom Brenner were always so dang enthusiastic, Patrick Regan appeared at just the right time with just the right words, and Christine Sumption kept telling me it was a good idea! Thanks to Nola Burger for showing me how to look at books, and nudging me always towards better design.

Keeping me on my toes, I recognize a new wave of healthy creative competition. In order of appearance: Olivia Morgan Heller, Samuel Payne Heller, Athos Argue, Annika Owenmark and Felix Dawans. The future looks bright with you in it.

Finally, my deep gratitude and respect to the superb craftspeople at Preiser GmbH, who have created such an extraordinary cast of characters and graciously permitted me to use them in my work.

Images in this collection are available as fine art prints.
Visit:

www.audreyheller.com

for a full gallery of available work, and a schedule of
exhibitions, events and adventures.

Published by Squint Pictures,
an imprint of Audrey Heller Photographs,
San Francisco, CA

Text and Photographs by Audrey Heller

Cover and design consultation by Jeff Raby

1st Edition

Introductory page: *Accent*, Thanks page: *Mine*

For permission to reproduce, purchasing
and distribution inquiries, please email:
books@squintpictures.com

Library of Congress Control Number: 2009901735

ISBN 9780979826306

Printed in Canada